# The Small Business Guide to Doing Payroll

## The Essential Guide to Understanding Payroll and What Software is Available to Help You

**Minute Help Guides**

www.minutehelp.com

# Table of Contents

# Introduction

If you own a small business with employees, you probably know how cumbersome, complicated and confusing payroll can be. Aspects of payroll such as social security, taxes, as well as state and federal payroll guidelines can make payroll seem overwhelming. This guide will show you the steps to do payroll for your small business effectively and efficiently. We'll cover how to do payroll using HR payroll software and payroll time clock software, as well as review some of the most popular payroll software packages on the market today.

# Chapter 1: Understanding How to Do Payroll

Payroll means two separate things when it comes to your small business. First off, payroll is the sum of your salaries, wages, bonuses as well as deductions. There's also payroll accounting, which refers to the amounts of money paid to regular employees for the job functions they perform for your business. Payroll accounting is a very important and often very confusing aspect of running a small business. It can severely affect your bottom line because of the taxes and other deductions that your business is subject to by state and federal agencies.

Sound payroll management means payroll irregularities are kept to a minimum, proper monies are deducted, and employees are paid on time. Companies that repeatedly experience payroll errors can suffer from low employee morale, frustration, and possible penalties and sanctions levied by state and federal officials.

# Payroll Taxes

If you are a small business owner you probably know how important it is to minimize tax liabilities while following the proper procedures and accounting standards. Government agencies at the local, state, and federal levels require small businesses to withhold income and payroll taxes. In the United States, income taxes and payroll taxes are separate. Payroll taxes fund government programs including Medicare, Medicaid, and Social Security.

Small businesses follow a basic formula to calculate net pay. Net pay is what is paid to the employee after payroll taxes are taken out of their respective checks. Gross pay is the amount of pay before all of the proper deductions have been taken out of the employee's check. Payroll taxes include the following:

Federal income tax withholding – these rates vary and are based on tables established by the United States Internal Revenue Service (IRS).

Social Security tax withholding – The employee pays 4.2% percent of their gross salary with the employer paying a little over six percent. Self-employed individuals are responsible for paying both sides, which adds up to a significant tax burden.

Medicare tax withholding – the total percentage that must be paid towards Medicare tax is 2.9% of gross pay. Like Social Security taxes, the sum is split into two equal percentages to be paid by the employee and the organization. In the case of Medicare tax withholding, the individual sums are 1.45%. Self-employed individuals are responsible for paying the entire 2.9%.

State income tax withholding – state income tax varies by state. 41 states have a state income tax while nine do not. The following states without state income tax are:

- Alaska
- Florida
- Nevada
- New Hampshire
- South Dakota
- Tennessee
- Texas
- Washington

- Wyoming

Small business owners have to pay additional payroll-related taxes above and beyond what the employee has to pay. In addition to Social Security and Medicare tax withholdings, the small business owner with employees must pay federal and state unemployment taxes. These tax contributions fund state and federal unemployment benefits to be distributed to those individuals who qualify for unemployment insurance benefits.

You've probably heard the term "FICA" used on occasions where payroll, wages, and taxes are discussed. FICA stands for Federal Insurance Contributions Act. The FICA tax includes the Social Security and Medicare taxes that are levied on business owners and employees. The sum of the FICA tax is 15.3%, which is shared by the employee and employer.

To provide consistency of cash flow and payments, small business owners generate their payroll distributions on a regular basis. This is also done so that employees can receive consistent payments in terms of when and how much. Most payrolls are done bi-weekly (every two weeks), semi-monthly (twice per month), and monthly. The most common intervals of time are bi-weekly and semi-monthly.

# Payroll Vocabulary

Part of the difficulty of understanding the payroll process is the array of vocabulary terms. Many small business owners know their own industry, products, and services like the back of their hands, but may not be familiar with accounting and tax-related words. To many small business owners, especially new ones, it's like trying to learn a foreign language. To help build a foundation of understanding when doing payroll, here is a list of commonly used words, along with their definitions.

# Salaries

Salaries are typically associated with more "white collar" occupations including office workers, managers, professionals and executives. Most people who are paid a salary receive payment on a semi-monthly basis, such as the middle and end of the month. Their earnings are usually stated in terms of gross pay (amount before any deductions are taken out).

# Wages

Wages are generally assigned to employees who work on a production-type basis. Hourly wages are generally assigned to more "blue collar"-type jobs. Most small business owners employ hourly wage workers for their services. The hourly rate of pay is stated in gross terms before any deductions are made. Hourly employee wages are generally paid on a weekly or bi-weekly basis. Payroll functions typically take more time for small businesses that employ hourly workers as opposed to salaried workers.

# Direct Deposit

Many employers pay their workers via direct deposit. This means that the funds are directly deposited into the employees' bank account from the employer's account without being withdrawn or having a check issued. The employee commonly receives a paper or electronic receipt from the employer with the details of the transaction. This saves money and speeds up the payroll process.

## Employee Identification Number

This number is used to identify corporations, organizations, partnerships, non-profits, and other non-individual entities. It is commonly referred to as an EIN number.

## Form W-2

This is an IRS form that must be completed for every employee that has income, Social Security, or Medicare taxes withheld from their pay.

# Overtime Pay

Overtime pay refers to hourly employee hours worked beyond 40 per week. Overtime pay is more per hour. The typical rate of overtime pay is known as "time and a half" or "double time." Salaried employees are usually exempt from receiving overtime pay even if they work more than 40 hours in a given work week.

# Chapter 2: How to Do Payroll

As most small business owners are aware, payroll is a necessary evil that is required when you have a small business that employs people. In this section we will show you a comprehensive overview of how to do payroll, which will serve as an excellent foundation before moving on to subsequent sections that discuss payroll tools you can use to do your payroll functions.

As stated earlier, payroll consists of much more than computing hours worked. Payroll consists of salaries, wages, bonuses, commissions, overtime payments, and payroll taxes. The employee and employer share the tax burden when paying payroll taxes such as Social Security, Medicare, federal and state income taxes. The small business owner must also include employer paid benefits into their payroll calculations including holidays, vacation, sick leave, insurance, and retirement plans. The above payroll accounts are those that appear on most small business owners' income statements and balance sheets.

# Calculating Payroll Withholdings

There are payroll withholdings that are withheld from an employees' gross pay as well as payroll withholdings that are not withheld from their wages/salary. The United States income tax structure requires that small business owners withhold payroll taxes. Much to the chagrin of most employees, these deductions reduce the amount of money they receive when they are paid for their services. These deductions also affect the employer in multiple ways by creating an accounting liability for the small business owner and requiring them to pay the money held back from employees' checks to the correct agencies within a certain timeframe.

As a small business owner you are responsible for the following employee payroll withholdings to be deducted from your employees' checks:

## Social Security

Medicare
Federal Income tax

State income tax (if applicable)
Court-ordered withholdings (garnishments, liens, etc.)

# Calculating Employee Social Security Tax

Many people debate the solvency and long-term liability of Social Security. Regardless of your stance on the issue, you are still required to deduct it from your employees' checks. Social Security and Medicare taxes make up what is known as FICA. The small business owner is required to pay their portion and deduct the employees' portion and pay it to the United States Federal Government.

As of 2011, the small business owner is required to withhold 4.2% of an employee's gross pay up to the amount of $106,800. Any money earned by an employee after this amount is not subject to Social Security tax. For example, if an employee earns an annual salary of $50,000, the employer is required to withhold 4.2% of this amount, which equates to $2,100 per year in Social Security tax withholdings.

If you have an employee that earns $200,000, only their salary up to $106,800 is subject to the Social Security tax withholdings. The rest is not subject to SS taxes.

In terms of payroll accounting, the amount withheld from the employee's check as well as the other portion that is to be paid by the employer is labeled as a liability until the amount is remitted to the United States government.

# Calculating Employee Medicare Tax

As previously mentioned, Medicare tax along with Social Security tax makes up FICA. Medicare tax is required by law to be withheld from an employees' gross pay, which is matched by the employer. This means that Medicare tax is an employee and employer expense that must be paid to the United States Government. As the small business owner, you are required to withhold 1.45% of each of your employees' annual wages for a combined total of 2.9%. Unlike Social Security tax, which is only levied against the first $106,800, Medicare taxes have no income limits. An employee earning an annual salary of $45,000 would have $1,305 withheld from their annual earnings.

# Calculating Federal Income Tax

Small business owners are also required to withhold a portion of money from their employees' earnings based upon their total annual salary/wages. The amount withheld is used to pay the employees' federal tax owed to the United States government. The amount is figured based on salary tables created by the Internal Revenue Service (IRS). Employees can manipulate this amount by indicating a specific number of withholding allowances on a W-4 form that can increase or decrease the amount of money withheld from their checks. The amount withheld is rarely the actual amount owed at the end of the tax year, which is why individuals have to pay the IRS more or are given a refund. Some employees that have a large number of exemptions or earn a very low wage are not required to pay federal income tax. Federal withholding amounts are recorded as accounting liabilities on your balance sheet until the amount is paid to the federal government.

# Calculating State Income Tax

41 of the 50 states have a state income tax. In those states it is the responsibility of the small business owner to deduct an estimated amount from the checks of their employees based on their salary/wages. Just like federal income tax, state income tax amounts can be increased or decreased by the employee based on their marital status and number of exemptions. State income taxes are recorded as a liability on your balance sheet until paid.

# Calculating Court-Ordered Withholdings

On some occasions a small business owner may be required to garnish the wages of an employee for various reasons. Court-ordered withholdings may include back-owed child support (arrears), and the payment of various debts. Court-ordered withholdings are typically a last resort after all other options have been exhausted. The amount of the garnishment is to be recorded as a liability on your small business's balance sheet.

# Other Withholdings

A small business may participate in other withholdings on a voluntary basis. These withholdings may include:

- Charitable contributions
- Retirement contributions
- Union dues

These voluntary withholdings are recorded in different ways depending on who the money goes to. If an outside agency is to receive the funds, the amount is recorded as a liability on the balance sheet. If the withholding goes to the employer the entry is not recorded as a liability because there is no remittance that takes place. It is then recorded as a credit to the employer.

# Employer Payroll Taxes, Costs and Benefits

As discussed earlier, employees and employers share the cost burden for many payroll associated expenses. We've covered how to properly deduct employee related payroll expenses and are ready to move on to employer expenses associated with payroll. Most small business people understand that salaries and wages are far from the only costs the employer must pay out when conducting their payroll operations. Below is a list of expenses that employers will incur that are related to payroll:

- Social Security tax – employer portion
- Medicare tax – employer portion
- Unemployment tax – state
- Unemployment tax – federal
- Worker's compensation tax
- Insurance – health, dental, life, disability
- Paid holidays, sick leave, vacation days
- Contributions to retirement plans, savings plans, profit sharing plans, pension plans
- Post-retirement health care

# Social Security Tax – Employer Portion

It is vital that you as a small business owner understand how to properly withhold your portion of Social Security tax. Remember, this is a shared expense paid for by the employee and employer. It is important to keep up with the latest regulations because these amounts do change on occasion. Prior to 2011 the employer and employee were required to contribute 6.2% each. In 2011, the employee contribution dropped to 4.2% while the employer portion remained at 6.2% of the first $106,800 of a worker's annual pay.

For example, if you have a project manager for your construction business that earns $60,000 a year you would deduct $2,520 from his or her total salary which equates to the 4.2% employee amount required to withhold. You would also have to remit $3,720 to the United States Federal government in order to meet the employer requirement of 6.2%. The total amount paid would be 10.4% or $6,240 for the year.

Let's say you have a high ranking employee you pay a salary of $150,000 per year. You would be required to withhold 4.2% of the first $106,800 of that person's salary which equals $4,485.60. The remaining amount above $106,800 is not subject to Social Security tax unless the law changes in the future. You, as the employer, would have to pay 6.2% which equals $6,621.60 for the year. It is important to record your (employer) portion as an expense and a current liability within your accounting documents until the amounts are paid.

## Medicare Tax – Employer Portion

All small business owners with employees must contribute a matching amount to the United States federal government. The amount, which must be equal to what your employee has withheld from his or pay, should be considered an expense to you. Currently the amount that must be paid by the employer is 1.45% of the employee's gross wages or salary. When it comes to Medicare tax there is no limit to the dollar amount that can be taxed unlike the Social Security tax.

Let's say you have an employee that earns an annual wage of $25,000 a year. You would withhold 1.45% of the total salary to meet the employee cost. You would then match that 1.45% to meet the employer cost. 1.45% of $25,000 equates to $362.50. The total amount paid for Medicare tax would be $725. Your share would be recorded as a current liability and an expense until the amount is paid to the internal Revenue Service (IRS).

# State Unemployment Tax

Up until now we've discussed several shared expenses that are paid by the employer and employee. State unemployment tax is not a shared expense, and is paid for in full by the employer. Unemployment tax rates are determined by each individual state. Not all businesses are required to pay state unemployment taxes. Some organizations such as places of worship and some non-profit organizations are exempt. It is up to you to contact your state unemployment office to determine what amount, if any, you should pay in state unemployment tax. State unemployment tax rates typically vary according to how much of a reserve the employer has built up in the unemployment state fund. If you have a large reserve your tax liability will typically be lower than if you have little or no reserves built up.

Most states only tax the first $7,000 in wages or salary. This may or may not be the amount for your particular state. Be sure to check with your state unemployment office to find out. Let's say your state's unemployment tax rate is 5%. That means for every employee on your payroll you would have to pay 5% of $7,000 or $350 each. Let's say that your small business has a total of four employees. Employee number one earned $24,000 in 2011, while employee number two earned $43,000. For each of those employees you would have to pay 5% of $7,000, which equals $350. Employees three and four were hired just recently and have only earned $5,000 and $6,000 in 2011. To calculate the amount of unemployment tax for employees three and four you would have to perform the following equations:

Employee 3: $5,000 x 5% = $250
Employee 4: $6,000 x 5% = $300

Remember that the employee does not pay any portion of the state unemployment tax. The entire amount is paid by the employer.

# Federal Unemployment Tax

The United States federal government supervises all of the state unemployment programs and thus requires employers to pay a federal unemployment tax of 0.8% on the initial $7,000 for each employee's wages or salary. For example, if you had an employee that earned $35,000 for 2011 you would be taxed at the rate of 0.8% of the first $7,000, which equals $56. Let's also assume you have a part-time employee that earned $5,500 during 2011. For that employee you would have to pay 0.8% of $5,500, which equates to $44. The entire portion of federal unemployment tax is paid for by you, the small business owner.

# Worker's Compensation Insurance Costs

Worker compensation insurance ensures that personnel who are injured on the job have compensation because of their injuries. Most states require that employers have worker's compensation insurance. The rates vary by state as well as other factors such as the type of business and industry, the job duties performed by the worker, and the claim history of the employer. For example, the worker's compensation rates can be as much as 15% for high risk jobs such as factory and construction workers. Conversely, worker's compensation insurance rates can be less than 1% of an employee's salary if they are an office worker.

To figure the premium for worker's compensation insurance the rate is applied to the employee's wages or salary. Even though the premium is calculated based on employee salary figures the employee does not pay any of the premium. 100% of the premium is paid for by the employer, and is factored into the employer's cost of doing business (overhead expenses). Each small business owner with employees should contact their state worker's compensation office for specific details.

As a small business owner you can pay the worker's compensation premium in advance if you would like. If you choose to pay the premium in advance you would record an asset in your accounting spreadsheet and reduce the asset while the worker's compensation expense increases as employees work. If you choose not to pay the premium in advance you must accrue the expense with an adjusting entry that notes the increase in worker's compensation insurance. Worker's compensation is a major expense for small business owners with employees and is therefore an important component of doing payroll.

## Insurance – Health, Dental, Life, Disability

In years past it was common for employers to provide insurance to their employees at little or no cost. That is simply not the reality for small business owners anymore. Escalating health care costs have caused employers to reduce or eliminate coverage while asking the employee to pay a larger portion of the premium out of their own pockets. The health care costs are so expensive that it is not uncommon for family coverage to cost over $1,000 a month. Because of skyrocketing costs, employers now require employees to pay a higher portion of the premium. The amount is usually collected from the employee through a payroll deduction each pay period. The net cost to the employer is simply the amount they pay minus the amount paid for by the employee.

# Paid holidays, sick leave, vacation days

Most small businesses pay their full-time, permanent employees for up to ten holidays per year. At a minimum, employees are usually paid for Christmas, New Year's, Memorial Day, 4th of July, Labor Day, and Thanksgiving. Most small businesses also give their employees one week's paid vacation after at least one year of employment. Paid sick leave is also a common benefit given to employees by small business owners. If the organization has an employee that is sick or has a medical issue they will be paid during their absence.

An accounting principle known as "The Matching Principle" states that the cost of paid holidays, vacation days, and sick days are to be recognized as an expense when the employee is working. In other words, the cost takes place when the employee earns the benefit rather than when the employee uses the benefit. For example, you have an employee that works the entire year of 2009 and therefore earns one week's paid vacation. During 2009, when the employee earned the benefit, is when you would record the expense. Let's say the employee takes the week's vacation in 2010. You would then reduce the liability of the company by debiting the vacation's payable account.

# Employer Contributions toward 401(K), Savings Plans, and Profit-Sharing Plans

Some small business owners contribute company funds to retirement and profit sharing plans. The small business owner is required to mark the contribution as a business expense during the period in which the employee earned the benefit.

# Contributions to Employee Pension Plans

Some small businesses offer pension plans that pay the employee after they retire. The cost of this benefit to the employer should be recorded and recognized during the time when the employee earns the pension benefits rather than when they actually receive the benefits.

Properly accounting for pension benefits can be confusing for some small business owners because the benefits are not used until after the employee has retired from the organization. To properly account for the entire cost of all benefits requires that you expense it while the employee is working in order to match the cost of the employee's work to the revenue earned as a result of their work.

## Retirement Health Insurance

Some small businesses continue to provide medical coverage for their employees after they retire. This is another benefit that is earned while the employee is still working, but not enjoyed until after he or she retires. Accrual accounting methods state that the future health insurance benefit be expensed as the employee earns the benefit while working as a member of your organization.

As you can see there are a lot of things to take into consideration when conducting payroll operations. As a small business owner it is critically important to keep up to date on information regarding these expenses because they can change at any time. Regardless if you choose to outsource your small business payroll tasks or do them yourself, it is important to have a solid foundation of understanding of how payroll works and how it affects your business's bottom line. In the next section we are going to evaluate some of the more popular payroll tools that are used by several small, medium, and large sized business organizations. These tools can greatly assist the small business owner to perform payroll duties on their own without having to hire additional personnel, leading to an increase in overhead expenses.

# Chapter 3: Using HR Payroll Software

## What is it?

When a business has employees, they must be paid for their work. HR Payroll software is a system that is designed to help the payroll or human resources departments automate the employee payment system and process. The software is designed to efficiently calculate and track a staff member's salary, wage, bonus, tax withholding, and deduction. This process of efficient automation can be expanded to include every employee associated with a business or company.

# How Much Does it Cost?

HR payroll software packages range in price depending on the system and its capabilities. The average cost is $150 - $3,000 per month or more. Most systems offer a free demo or trial period and are presented on a subscription only basis. The larger the company, the more the system costs.

# Pros

One of the greatest benefits for human resources departments using HR payroll software is that it can calculate pre-configured and complex calculations that would normally take a human a lengthy amount of time to complete. Heads of departments or payroll personnel find that they have more time to focus on other aspects of their job when using this type of software because it automates and configures otherwise cumbersome tasks. HR payroll software can be used to calculate the hours worked by staff automatically, as well as configure a staff member's salary and benefits. This in itself saves time and money.

Some HR payroll software can aid in the projection of costs and savings for a business or organization. Future staff costs can be predicted, which enables a business to create realistic budgets that are highly effective and more likely to be adhered to. Cost savings is an important key to success for businesses, especially smaller organizations that do not have a lot of room to move. Businesses that are able to create effective budgets that are more realistic to the spending projections of the company are more likely to stick to them over time. The more a company is able to stick to the budget, the better it will function as a whole and enable employees to increase their productivity in the business.

Automation seems to be the biggest benefit with using HR payroll software. From calculating and tracking employee wages to generating annual payroll tax, this software can automate just about any payroll process. Not only do the payroll software systems print paychecks, but some generate tax-related reports and forms as well. These forms can be helpful for both the managers and employees. Tax withholdings and Worker's Compensation fees can also be calculated and taken out. In fact, some systems calculate figures and log them into the appropriate categories or accounts. The entire process can be streamlined, making payroll a much simpler and more efficient duty than completing it manually.

Improved organization is a key benefit to using HR payroll software. Not only are paychecks and taxes calculated and withheld correctly, but payroll records and reports are nicely consolidated and organized into neat and tidy categories for future referencing. Management reports are also improved by tracking the amount of labor paid by the job, account or even cost center. All of the payroll systems are categorized and organized the way the human resource department desires so that reports can be run or reviewed when needed. Improved organization helps the company stay on task when tax time arrives as well as keep organized all year round. The organization makes the company more efficient and department heads spend less time crunching numbers and determining labor costs.

# Cons

While most companies that offer HR payroll software promise a seamless integration, this does not always happen. There can be glitches and kinks that need to be worked out on early integration of the system. When inputting numbers or formulas into the program, at set-up, an error can occur which throws the calculations off. It is best to try to be as systematic as possible when setting the system up to avoid problems. In the event that an error does occur, good HR payroll software companies offer customer service to assist with problems.

The learning curve can be somewhat steep, especially for 'old hats' that have been manually cutting paychecks for decades. It can be difficult to trust the capabilities of a system that takes all of the control of a payroll department and puts it into practice. Relinquishing control can be a difficult task. Most have found that the early months of implementation can be rough for some department heads, but the payroll and human resource departments welcome the change as time goes on.

# Who is it a Good Idea for?

HR payroll software can be used by a business of nearly any size, as long as that company has employees. There is no sense in using payroll software if the company has no employees to pay. Larger companies benefit greatly by using an automated system for payroll because of the time saved and minimization of errors when completing the payroll process.

Also, payroll is a date that cannot be missed – no matter what else is going on in the business. The payroll date is typically why most people show up for work in the first place; they want to be paid for their hard work. Timely and accurate payment systems are critical to any sized business. Late payroll payments or delayed tax withholdings can be detrimental to a business, causing financial penalties. It is important that the date be adhered to no matter the size of the company or how busy the human resources department is. HR payroll software is designed to keep any company on track in terms of payroll and tax withholdings. Payroll software ensures that the employee is paid on time and the amount is accurate.

Any sized company can benefit from using HR payroll software. The system is designed to save organization's time and money, both presently and in the future. There are a wide number of systems available and it pays to complete the research beforehand in order to find the best suited software.

# Chapter 4: Using Payroll Time Clock Software

## What is it?

Payroll time clock software is designed to manage and track staff time in an efficient and highly automated fashion. Whether you operate a small, medium or large sized business or organization, payroll time clock software provides secure tools for determining who is and is not working and what hours they complete.

The features are sophisticated and the system is secure. Accurate employee time can be calculated without making mistakes. The systems vary in features but are all designed with one goal in mind – to eliminate human error associated with time tracking for employees on spreadsheets and punch cards. Payroll time clock software implements an automated system that includes work schedules, attendance, job costing and processing payroll. Data entry is minimized, which leads to less time spent inputting information into the computer and less room for error.

## How Much Does it Cost?

Cost varies depending on system. The typical cost range of a payroll time clock software system is $59.95 - $149.99. Most software systems offer a 30 day free trial.

# Pros

There are a number of pros associated with using payroll time clock software, the first of which is that the software is designed to eliminate those tedious and manual procedures attached to payroll. Tedious tasks that have to be done every day can be eliminated by fully automating the payroll system and reporting through the time clock software. You are able to implement your own payroll rules and configure the software to read exactly what you need it to.

Payroll production costs can be lowered by implementing a payroll time clock software system. The system is highly accurate and seamlessly integrates into the daily routine of the business, allowing management to obtain more control over the payroll and time reporting system. Business operations become managed better because there is less room for error and fudging numbers. If an hourly employee shows up fifteen minutes late for work, they are docked for those fifteen minutes because they will clock-in at the accurate time. There is no time lost by the business during unproductive hours.

The integration of the system is one of the most positive aspects of using payroll time clock software in a business or organization. Most valuable software systems integrate seamlessly with little effort on that of the Human Resources or Payroll departments. Payroll applications are typically seamless as well. For smaller businesses that do not have an in-house payroll department, time sheets can be printed from an outsourced department for each employee to be paid. The software is designed to calculate to the minute the amount of time the employee has worked, so that the checks are accurately calculated. In most cases, businesses save money due to the high level of accuracy and seamless integration offered by the software systems.

For small companies, every penny matters in terms of cutting costs. With a payroll time clock software system in place, a small business can take advantage of monitoring employee attendance. Businesses can cut back on paying time out for non-working hours. Hours spent on the job are accurately calculated so that the business does not overpay for time not worked.

# Cons

Most businesses that implement the payroll time clock software reporting system claim few to no cons associated with the integration. However, there is somewhat of a learning curve for employees when getting started. Employees may forget to clock-in because they are not used to doing it. In this case, more work must be done from the human resources department. Employees may forget to clock-out at lunch or even back in after a break, in which case more paperwork must be done to ensure the employee gets paid for the time worked. Educational workshops and printed instructions help employees remember to initiate the new system.

Other cons associated with the implementation of the payroll time clock software system arise when the system is down or malfunctions. Most companies that provide these types of services offer a back-up plan in the event that the system is down, but during this time problems can arise. The in-house human resources or payroll departments may become bombarded with paperwork and handwritten time sheets in the event that the system crashes. Even one day of mix-up can create a large amount of work for those involved.

Correcting mistakes made by employees who clock-in late or even early is a common complaint of users of the payroll time clock system. There is no room for error and if an employee clocks in late they typically will not be paid for the time missed unless they involve management or human resources. Additional paperwork must be filled out and processed in order for the time missed to count. This can be troublesome for both the employee and the manager. Additional work is then required for the person who must input the information or override existing time worked into the system. In a large company with hundreds or thousands of employees, mistakes can routinely be made leaving a large amount of paperwork processing for managers.

## Who is it a Good Idea for?

A payroll time clock software system is good for all sized businesses, from small to large. Organizations of all sizes benefit from the accuracy that comes from using the system. The accuracy in time reporting helps cut costs at even the most basic level in even the smallest of organizations.

Large organizations seem to gain the most benefit from the system software due to the large number of employees and productivity that needs to be monitored. There is no accurate way for a payroll or human resources department to read through time sheets and process the information manually. The payroll time clock software system allows the company to become more automated in their reporting system and reap the benefits of accuracy and cost savings. While small companies may benefit from the system, larger companies typically have more overhead and production costs, thus the impact on savings is greater.

# Chapter 5: Using Form Plus Software

## What is it?

Form plus software is a system designed to automate the forms your business uses on a regular basis. These system software packages may include ready-made forms that can be customized to fit your business needs, or allow your company the flexibility to create your own professional form with personally designed themes and information that is needed on the form.

Small to large businesses, in nearly every niche or sector, can benefit from a form plus software package that saves the company time and money. Common templates include medical and legal forms, purchase orders, bid proposals, employee time cards, expense reports, fax cover sheets, memos, invoice forms and more. Tax forms are also included in some form plus software systems and include an automated way to print onto pre-printed or blank paper tax forms.

## How Much Does it Cost?

Free demonstrations and trial periods are typically offered by form plus software companies. The software is typically paid on a subscription basis monthly and ranges anywhere between $49/month and $15,000/month depending on the package and size of the business.

# Pros

One of the major benefits of using form plus software is time savings. Not only do you eliminate the time spent filling out forms, but in most cases you will never run out of the forms; you'll just have to wait for the printer to deliver another batch. You can simply print the forms yourself with the automated system set-up on the office computer. Ready-to-use forms can be accessed electronically from the PC. There is no longer a waiting period for tax forms from the IRS or medical forms from Medicare, the forms can be accessed for immediate use.

Form completion is another benefit of using form plus software. From payroll tax forms to internal memos, forms can be pre-filled out so that you do not have to complete the forms by hand. The time savings can be immense depending on what form you are filling out. For tax forms, data and calculations can be extracted from the payroll systems and entered directly onto the form. There is no time spent completing a tax form by hand because everything that is needed is directly entered onto the form.

Not only does a company save time using form plus software, no matter what the form, money is also saved because of the elimination of human error. Some of the most time consuming and work intensive forms can be automated online, and information inputted prior to printing. This will eliminate manual error that can occur when an individual must complete the form by hand.

Other benefits of using form plus software include the flexibility in creating the form as intelligent as you need it to be. Arithmetic formulae can be added to the text fields whether binding or repetitive filing to ensure accuracy and efficiency. There is no more room for human error from manually putting the numbers into the system. By using a form plus software system, numbers or calculations can be set up to ensure that the right formula is being used to generate the correct data. This automated system can be linked to report generation to ensure that month or year-end reporting is accurate and effective. This feature exhibits a large time savings benefit for those involved in inputting data. Time can be spent on other tasks and the form generation can be left to the computer. Electronic forms can be made highly intelligent by setting up the formulae before using.

As previously mentioned, current data from the forms can be exported into a CSV file which can then be imported to Microsoft Excel or other spreadsheet documents for easy reading and referencing. The exporting of data saves money because time can be spent on other tasks, while the software takes care of exporting the necessary data needed to generate reports. The benefits are great in using form plus software for your business.

# Cons

As with most automated software systems, integration can be a huge headache for department heads and those directly involved with the implementation of form plus software. Converting the forms over to automated means can take time and effort, but once the system is up and running the software is highly efficient. In the meantime, getting the precise look and feel of the form takes time and patience.

While the form plus software promises a large savings over time, the initial cost of implementing the system can be costly. For companies like large medical centers, legal outfits, and hospitals, the cost upfront may be thousands of dollars to implement the system due to the large number of forms that need to be converted. However, the efficiency of having the forms automated does save time and money over the long haul.

## Who is it a Good Idea for?

Form plus software is designed for any sized company that uses forms on a regular basis. Whether a business has few employees or hundreds, automated form plus software can provide benefits, by saving time, money and work. If the business uses a large number of paper forms, the original form can be converted into an electronic form by scanning or importing the information.

Even the busiest of offices, companies can benefit from using the form plus software. Most software companies that offer this type of product also offer free online support. Comprehensive user's manuals are offered but many department managers benefit from the online support that is available at your disposal. The customer service is there to aid in set-up, transition or use of the form processing. In the event that there is an issue, companies can rest assured that help is available and you are not on your own once the contract is signed.

Any company that uses forms on a regular basis, whether internally or externally, can greatly benefit from using form plus software. The design of the software is to save small and large businesses time and money on both the front and back-ends.

# Chapter 6: Using Payroll Plus Software

## What is it?

Payroll plus software incorporates the latest in technology and makes the art of processing payroll a simple and efficient task that can be incorporated in-house rather than outsourcing the system. A small business or large company no longer has to rely on outsourced services to process their payroll when using payroll plus software. The task can be done in-house to save time and money.

Most payroll plus software includes the basic payroll processing system that allows you to complete standard payroll calculations as well as other operations and capabilities. Time recording, reporting, personnel records storage and planning are some of the other features attached to the payroll plus software.

With the time recording features, payroll systems can be linked up to timesheet reporting systems that compile information about the hours worked by an employee. This information is then automatically transferred to the payroll system to make calculating payroll that much simpler and more efficient.

## How Much Does it Cost?

A reliable supplier should be selected before implementing payroll plus software. Most suppliers offer a free trial period and a subscription basis. Some systems, depending on the capabilities and features may run anywhere between $39/month to several thousand dollars per month.

# Pros

One of the most talked about benefits of using payroll plus software is the planning and forecasting it allows for the business. Some payroll software packages include forecasting features that allow you plan staffing costs, employee wages and realistic budgets. Hypothetical numbers can be entered into the system to determine estimates or exact numbers projected to be spent or saved. The exact cost of an employee can be determined by using this type of software.

With some payroll plus software packages, more than simple payroll processing can be done. Many organizations and larger companies utilize other software packages to keep track of employee records, such as annual leave, sick time, or vacation breaks. With the payroll plus software, these recordings may be kept within one software package. You no longer need additional types of software packages to keep track of this information. It can be stored and retrieved through the payroll plus software. Storing personnel records is simple and highly efficient when using this type of software. Also, the system is highly secure so that sensitive records are kept safe and protected from those who do not have the authority to review the information.

Through the time recording system provided on payroll plus software, payroll data can be provided in a number of helpful reports. An in-depth analysis of payroll spending, staff costs, department costs, jobs and contracts, and even business costs can be reviewed. The reports can be run at any time during the month or year. Year-end and monthly reports can also be created to review costs and savings. As previously stated, projected costs and realistic budget planning keeps the business ahead of the game and allows savings to be implemented as needed. By saving money overall in the business, the payroll plus software is worth its weight in gold. Not only do you save money upfront, but through the course of the year by using the system.

Year-end reporting is automated and all of the information, including pay slips, is archived in the system. This convenient way of archiving reports and information is helpful in the event that copies are needed at a later date. Employee records can be stored in the event that staff needs to receive copies or the IRS asks to see further information. This is a huge benefit of the payroll plus software because information is never lost or misplaced, but always accessible.

# Cons

Implementation of the payroll plus software can be time consuming and in some cases offers a major learning curve. If a company has been doing the same payroll procedures for years, the new changes can be difficult to get used to. This is especially true of human resource or payroll departments who are used to doing things their way and are adverse to change.

The integration of the system may require that current computer systems in the business be updated. Most payroll plus software packages are compatible with a variety of operating systems, but in the event that the computer system is antiquated, it may be time to upgrade. If an upgrade is necessary, the implementation can be costly because new computers and software packages are needed in order for the payroll plus software to work appropriately. If the upgrade is not in the budget, a business may have to hold off on implementing the system until projected costs can be absorbed.

There is some work to be done in processing payroll each month. During this time, reporting must be accurate and the system ran by trained individuals within the company. If a business is used to outsourcing this work, they will need to train an in-house person or department to stay on top of the payroll system and ensure that it is done timely and effectively. While the software is designed to make the process easy and simple, there is still work to be done – especially if a company has never completed the process in-house.

## Who is it a Good Idea for?

Payroll plus software can be used for nearly every company or organization that has employees. If the business has one or 3,000 employees, the software system is designed to help. No matter what age the business is, payroll plus software can be incorporated. Whether the company is starting from the ground up or has been in business for years, payroll plus software can be used.

A business looking to cut costs on outsourcing their payroll operation can greatly benefit from using an in-house payroll plus software package. Training, education and support are available from the right supplier, and the software is designed to save your business time and money over the long haul. Outsourcing can be expensive and most companies who have transitioned to payroll plus software report a large savings over time.

# Chapter 7: Using QuickBooks Software

## What is it?

QuickBooks software is perhaps the most widely known accounting software on the market today. QuickBooks is made by the software company Intuit. Millions of small business owners use QuickBooks for their accounting needs. There are several different versions of QuickBooks including QuickBooks Online Simple, Online Essentials, Online Plus, Pro, Premier, for Mac, Accountant, and Enterprise Solutions.

No matter what QuickBooks version you use, it is tailor made to handle small business financial tasks. QuickBooks was created after Intuit's initial success with the personal financial software Quicken. Scott Cook and Tom Proulx, founders of Intuit, designed QuickBooks for small business owners who had no formal accounting training. They realized that small business people were often lacking in accounting know-how. The software quickly established market dominance by capturing over 85% of the small business marketplace. Today, some industry statistics show that QuickBooks has a nearly 95% market share in the small business accounting software category.

## How Much Does it Cost?

Because there are so many versions of QuickBooks software, the costs vary greatly. For example, QuickBooks Online is the simplest version and can be purchased for as little as $12.95 per month after a free 30 day trial offer. QuickBooks Enterprise Solution, which is the company's most robust version, costs approximately $600 per user, and is made for large organizations with multiple employees and locations. QuickBooks for Mac, Pro, and Premier cost $229.95 and $399.95 respectively.

# Pros

One of the main benefits of QuickBooks is that it comes with New User Setup that includes coaching tips on how to get started using QuickBooks. One of the main reasons QuickBooks was able to establish market dominance was that it was created for the small business person with no accounting background. Intuit has kept up this great feature in all of its iterations of QuickBooks, including the most recent versions.

QuickBooks allows small business owners to keep track of all of their financial records in one place. It also provides a big picture prospective for the business owner via the QuickBooks Homepage. This portal shows how all of the major financial categories and tasks fit together to make your business operate. The main tasks are automatically organized by groups such as customers, suppliers, vendors, and financial institutions. The homepage also uses flow charts to display how each financial task relates to the other, which helps you decide on which task to do next.

One of the biggest challenges small business owners face is tracking their finances throughout the complete business cycle from sale to collection. QuickBooks easily creates invoices for billing vendors and customers, which allows you to save a lot of time. The intuitive interface keeps invoices, bills, and payments all in one location. QuickBooks allows you to access all of this information with just a few clicks of a mouse.

With QuickBooks, tax time does not have to be a record keeping nightmare. The accounting software organizes your data so that come tax time it's easy to find reliable records to complete your taxes. QuickBooks has a one-click tax report function that uses all of the proper data and creates a completed tax form in just one click. The record keeping functions also help you drill down on data to analyze your business. The data can easily be exported to Excel for further data analysis.

Another major challenge for small businesses is keeping track and organizing customer, employee and vendor data. QuickBooks has data centers with all of the important data that you need. For example, the customer center compiles all of the pertinent customer data into one location that can be used for reports and research.

With QuickBooks, you can also quickly and easily get a snapshot of your business's overall health. The snapshot feature gives you a glance at important business data such as year-over-year revenue, expenses, income, and even your best customers.

QuickBooks strives to stay on the cutting edge of technology and convenience. One of the great features that incorporate these two characteristics is the paperless banking feature that allows you to safely download banking transactions into your QuickBooks. That means you will save tons of time by not having to manually type in transactions. This one feature alone makes QuickBooks worth the price.

QuickBooks' ease of use and scalability makes seemingly insurmountable accounting tasks quick and easy. Investing in QuickBooks means you do not have to outsource accounting tasks to expensive CPAs or hire an additional staff member to do your books. Small business owners have to be very conscience of their bottom line and that means cutting down on personnel costs as much as possible without sacrificing performance and accuracy. Performing accounting functions and duties looms like a dark cloud over the heads of many small business owners because of the complexity of rules and abundance of data. QuickBooks makes it quick, simple and organized.

# Cons

QuickBooks has many more pros than cons, but there are a few shortcomings. For example, the Pro version does not store inventory location information. It also does not support the cost methods of First In First Out (FIFO) or Last In First Out (LIFO) methods.

Another common complaint about QuickBooks is that there are too many versions, making it difficult for small business professionals to know which version would be the best one for them. Small business owners with no background in accounting may find it difficult to decipher which version would be best for them. The most popular versions are the Pro and Premier versions, which are used by new and established businesses of various sizes.

# Who is it a Good Idea for?

QuickBooks is a great financial software and accounting solution for businesses of all sizes and types. The plethora of choices may make it somewhat confusing for small business owners to choose, but it also means there will be a version that is perfect for all of your financial needs. No matter if you have an organization of one or 1,000 – QuickBooks will have a tailored software package for you.

# Conclusion

Payroll is one of those necessary evils that go along with owning a business that has grown to the point of needing employees. We hope that after reading this guide you have a better understanding of what the payroll process is all about, and that you learned about some helpful financial tools that are available to the small business person. The rules and procedures surrounding payroll can seem confusing at first, so we encourage you to read through this guide more than once. With a little practice and the right payroll tools you'll be a payroll pro in no time.

# About Minute Help Press

Minute Help Press is building a library of books for people with only minutes to spare. Follow @minutehelp on Twitter to receive the latest information about free and paid publications from Minute Help Press, or visit minutehelp.com.